Kelli Broers
Cornelia & Jean Unite

LaunchCrate Publishing
Kansas City, KS

Illustrated by
Gilbert Emuge

Cornelia & Jean Unite
Written by Kelli Broers
Illustrated by Gilbert Emuge

© 2021 LaunchCrate Publishing

ALL RIGHTS RESERVED. No part of this publication may be reproduced, distributed, or transmitted in any form or by any means, including photocopying, recording, or other electronic or mechanical methods, without the prior written permission of the publisher, except in the case of brief quotations embodied in critical reviews and certain other noncommercial uses permitted by copyright law. For permission requests, email the publisher with subject "Attention: Permissions Coordinator," at the email address below.

LaunchCrate Publishing
Kansas City, KS
info@launchcrate.com
www.launchcrate.com

Ordering Information:
Quantity sales. Special discounts are available on quantity purchases by corporations, associations, and others. For details, contact the publisher at the email address above. Orders by U.S. trade bookstores and wholesalers.

Library of Congress Control Number: 2020923147

ISBN: 978-1-947506-21-3 (Hardcover)

Printed in the United States of America
10 9 8 7 6 5 4 3 2 1

First Edition

For my grandmothers—whose resilience, loyalty, and love endure.

Cornelia the porcupine was crying.
No one wanted to be her friend for very long.
She wasn't soft like a puppy or kitten.

When she became scared, she sent her quills flying.

She couldn't help it. It was the way God made her.

It helped to keep her safe, but it made keeping friends difficult.

When she became scared, she perfumed the air with a foul smelling odor.

She couldn't help it. It was the way God made her.

Her smell helped to keep her safe,

but it made keeping friends difficult.

 Cornelia was moping through the forest feeling sad and sorry for herself.
And then she smelled it.
The stinkiest smell she had ever smelled.

 She started to waddle the opposite direction when she heard crying. Someone was sad. Cornelia turned around and walked back to the stink.

The crying became louder.

"Boo hoo. Boo hoo."

Big, giant sobs.

"You are sad!
I'm not going anywhere," Cornelia said.
"Why are you crying?"

"Because when I get scared, I smell.
And no one wants to be friends with me," sniffled Jean.

"I'll be friends with you.

My name is Cornelia

and no one wants to be friends with me

because when I get scared,

I send my quills flying."

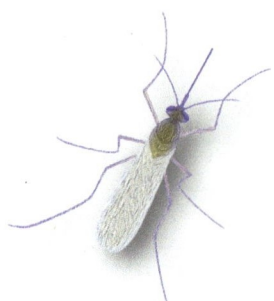

"I'm Jean. Nice to meet you."

They both began to giggle.

And off through the forest

the unlikely pair went.

They sang songs and shared stories.

Best of all, they liked to lay down in the meadow and take long naps in the sunshine.

But one sunny day,
while Cornelia and Jean softly snored during
an afternoon nap,
a big, shaggy coyote was looking for a snack.

Cornelia and Jean looked delicious.
He creeped up slowly, slowly, even more slowly.
He was barely moving. He froze and waited.

He jumped at them.

Jean turned her bottom towards the coyote

and sprayed everything she had.

The coyote's eyes burned and he began to cry!

Cornelia released her quills and hit the coyote in the face.

The coyote yelped, turned tail, and ran away. He would have to find his snack somewhere else.

Cornelia and Jean were relieved.

They hugged each other tight.

Thank goodness they were friends.

Together, they had saved the day.

About the Illustrator

Gilbert Opolot Emuge was born to Dr. James Emuge and Rev. Annah Francis Emuge in a small and poor town named Serere, Uganda, located on the eastern side of the continent of Africa. He moved to the United States when he was 3 years of age and he grew up in St. Charles, Missouri. Gilbert took an interest in art when he was in grade school. A neighbor taught him how to draw and he was hooked. After high school, he earned a Bachelor of Fine Arts in Graphic Design at Missouri State University. Gilbert has worked in television as a graphic designer in the Midwest and on the west coast.

Kelli Broers is a lifelong Kansan, a lover of the outdoors, and a mom who loves to read to kids. She is passionate about literacy and the possibilities it provides. She wrote this story with the hopes that it will encourage children to embrace all of their talents— even those that might be framed as a weakness by others. And just as importantly, she hopes it will help them embrace their peers, just as they are.

About the Author

CPSIA information can be obtained
at www.ICGtesting.com
Printed in the USA
LVHW071959160321
681668LV00037B/1383